Imagine 6

WORKBOOK

Katherine Stannett

Mary Charrington

COURSE CONSULTANTS

Elaine Boyd

Paul Dummett

T0349570

NATIONAL GEOGRAPHIC LEARNING

Australia • Brazil • Canada • Mexico • Singapore • United Kingdom • United States

National Geographic Learning,
a Cengage Company

Imagine 6 Workbook

Authors: Katherine Stannett, Mary Charrington

Course Consultants: Elaine Boyd, Paul Dummett

Publisher: Rachael Gibbon

Executive Editor: Joanna Freer

Project Manager: Natalie Roberts

Editorial Assistant: Polly McLachlan

Director of Global Marketing: Ian Martin

Product Marketing Manager: Fernanda De Oliveira

Heads of Strategic Marketing:

  Charlotte Ellis (Europe, Middle East and Africa)

  Justin Kaley (Asia and Greater China)

  Irina Pereyra (Latin America)

Senior Content Project Manager: Beth McNally

Senior Media Researcher: Leila Hishmeh

Senior Art Director: Brenda Carmichael

Operations Support: Rebecca G. Barbush, Hayley Chwazik-Gee

Manufacturing Manager: Eyvett Davis

Composition: Composure

For permission to use material from this text or product,
submit all requests online at **cengage.com/permissions**
Further permissions questions can be emailed to
permissionrequest@cengage.com

ISBN: 978-0-357-91187-7

National Geographic Learning
Cheriton House, North Way,
Andover, Hampshire, SP10 5BE
United Kingdom

Locate your local office at **international.cengage.com/region**

Visit National Geographic Learning online at **ELTNGL.com**
Visit our corporate website at **www.cengage.com**

Printed in the United Kingdom by Ashford Colour Press
Print Number: 01 Print Year: 2022

Imagine **6** WORKBOOK

A Circle the correct answer.

Minna: What ¹· *do you do / are you doing* right now, Felix?

Felix: I ²· *play / 'm playing* the drums.

Minna: ³· *Do you play / Are you playing* the drums every day?

Felix: Yes, ⁴· *I do / I am.* I want to be really good. ⁵· *Do you like / Are you liking* music?

Minna: Yes, ⁶· *I do / I am*, but I prefer sports. I ⁷· *go / 'm going* cycling three times a week. I ⁸· *don't do / 'm not doing* any exercise today, though.

Felix: Why not?

Minna: I've got lots of homework! I ⁹· *finish / 'm finishing* my history project.

B Circle the word that doesn't fit in each group.

1. **Food:**	broccoli	courgette	towel
2. **Technology:**	laptop	e-book	soap
3. **Musical instruments:**	cello	drums	airport
4. **Buildings:**	jam	floor	roof

C Complete the email with the words from the box.

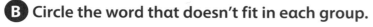

classical   concert   kayaking   nervous   restaurant   university

Dear Uncle Ted,

I'm having a great holiday! Yesterday we went ¹· _____ in the river. I was a bit ²· _____ at first, but I really enjoyed it. We had lunch at a little ³· _____ by the river, and then we visited an old ⁴· _____ . It was very beautiful and more than two hundred years old! In the evening we went to a ⁵· _____ and listened to some music by Mozart. I don't usually like ⁶· _____ music, but this was wonderful.

Hope you are well!
Tomas

Send

D Tick the sentences about the past. Then rewrite the other sentences in the past simple.

1. Did you see Carla at the party? _____

2. They throw the ball into the swimming pool. _____

3. She doesn't write in her notebook. _____

4. We went to school at eight o'clock. _____

5. Do you like the concert? _____

6. I didn't send a text to you. _____

7. My friends and I go horse riding. _____

8. He ate a banana for breakfast. _____

They threw the ball into the swimming pool.

_____

_____

_____

E Listen to Sonya and Jun. Then read the sentences. Write T (true) or F (false). 🎧 TR: 0.1

1. Sonya played football in her garden at home. _____

2. Sonya and her brother had ice cream. _____

3. In the afternoon, Sonya played with her cousins. _____

4. She made some bread with her aunt. _____

5. Jun and his mum planted some seeds in their garden. _____

6. They ate some strawberries for lunch. _____

F What did you do last weekend? Write six sentences. Describe things you did and things you didn't do. Use the phrases in the box or your own ideas.

eat ice cream	go cycling	go shopping	help in the garden
listen to music	play with friends	read a book	watch TV

On Saturday morning, I went shopping with my dad. I didn't play with my friends.

_____

_____

_____

Lesson 1 Vocabulary

A Circle the correct answer.

1.

prize / rider

2.

race / prize

3.

stadium / prize

4.

stadium / winner

5.

winner / competition

6.

rider / competition

B Listen to the conversation. Answer the questions. 🎧 TR: 1.1

1. What did Marek do last weekend?

_____

2. Where was it?

_____

3. How many races did Marek run in?

_____

4. How many races did Marek win?

_____

5. What was his prize?

_____

C Design a poster for a competition at your school. Answer these questions:

1. What type of competition is it?

2. When / Where is it?

3. What do you have to do?

4. How do you win?

5. What are the prizes?

A **Look at the table.** Write about what the people were or weren't doing yesterday.

Noora	have lunch	do homework	sleep
Khalid and Hamad	play football	visit their aunt	watch TV
Me	_____	_____	_____

1. Noora / play football / at four o'clock

   Noora wasn't playing football at four o'clock. _____

2. Khalid and Hamad / watch TV / at nine o'clock

   _____

3. Noora / have lunch / at twelve o'clock

   _____

4. Khalid and Hamad / do homework / at twelve o'clock

   _____

B **Complete the table from Activity A about yourself.** Write two sentences about what you were doing and two sentences about what you weren't doing.

I was reading a book at twelve o'clock. I wasn't sleeping at four o'clock. _____

_____

_____

_____

C **Complete the questions with the past continuous.** Then match the questions (1–5) with the answers (a–e).

1. What _____ (your sister / read) last night?
2. _____ (you / use) your computer at nine o'clock?
3. Who _____ (you / talk to) in the playground?
4. Why _____ (he / smile)?
5. What _____ (they / do) in the park?

a. Playing football.
b. My cousin.
c. A book about chess.

d. Yes, I was.
e. Because he was happy.

A **Scan the text.** Circle the correct answers to complete the summary. Then listen.

It's very ¹· *difficult / easy* to climb Mount Kilimanjaro. Chaeli reached the top in a wheelchair with Team ²· *Great / Awesome*. It ³· *was / wasn't* a very big challenge, and it took three ⁴· *months / years* to plan everything. Chaeli's message is that it's OK to be ⁵· *the same / different*.

A Different Kind of Expedition 🎧 TR: 1.2

Chaeli Mycroft is from South Africa. In September 2016, she was one of the thousands of people who attempted to **reach** the top of Mount Kilimanjaro, in Tanzania, the highest mountain in Africa. She did it along with her team, Team **Awesome**. Reaching the summit of Kilimanjaro wasn't easy. For most people, it's difficult to **breathe** at 2,000 metres and higher. Mount Kilimanjaro is 5,895 metres high. Every step of the way, the air gets thinner. An extra challenge for Chaeli was that she uses a wheelchair as she was born with cerebral palsy. This didn't stop her from trying to climb the highest mountain in Africa.

Chaeli had a custom-built, lightweight wheelchair made for the **expedition**. Her seven team members, also known as the 'Chaeli Kili Climbers' helped her climb up to the top in five days and get down again in two days. It took almost three years to plan the expedition, and Chaeli had to **train** for three months in a chamber with thin air so that she could learn how to breathe differently. The message that Chaeli wanted to send out to the world is that 'it's OK to be different. You can work together to make something beautiful happen.'

B **Read the text again.** Complete the sentences with information from the text.

1. Chaeli climbed Mount Kilimanjaro in _____.

2. It was a difficult trip because Chaeli uses a _____.

3. It took _____ to plan Chaeli's trip.

4. Chaeli had to train in a chamber with _____.

C **Complete the sentences with the words from the box.**

| awesome | breathe | ~~expedition~~ | gave up | reach | sign | trained |

1. Chaeli went on an exciting ___expedition___ to Mount Kilimanjaro.

2. She _____ hard, and she never _____.

3. People _____ the top of Kilimanjaro and take photos next to a _____.

4. It's hard to _____ on the summit, but the view is _____!

A Match to form sentences.

1. We were playing football
2. When I called him
3. Who were you talking to
4. She was running in a race
5. Were the students working
6. He was making a cake

a. when I saw you at the party yesterday?
b. when we kicked the ball through the window.
c. when their teacher came into the classroom?
d. when he dropped an egg.
e. he was reading a magazine in the park.
f. when she fell and hurt her leg.

B Complete the sentences with the past simple or past continuous form of the verbs in parentheses.

1. We __were listening__ (listen) to music when the cat _____jumped_____ (jump) out of the window.

2. They _____ (race) towards us when one rider _____ (fall) off his horse.

3. When I _____ (come) into the room, my brother _____ (sing) loudly.

4. What _____ (you / do) when we _____ (call) you at six o'clock yesterday?

5. He _____ (walk) to school when it _____ (start) to rain.

C Listen to the conversation. Then correct sentences 1–5 with the words from the box. 🎧 TR: 1.3

> do homework   ~~not watch~~   talk on her phone
> visit her aunt   walk to work

1. Joe watched the tennis match on TV yesterday.

   Joe didn't watch the tennis match on TV yesterday.

2. Joe was visiting his aunt yesterday afternoon.

   Joe _____ yesterday afternoon.

3. Sophie was talking on her phone yesterday afternoon.

   Sophie _____ yesterday afternoon.

4. Sophie's aunt was driving to work when she fell.

   Sophie's aunt _____ when she fell over.

5. She was waving to a friend and didn't see the banana peel.

   She _____ and didn't see the banana peel.

A **Read the short story and complete the chart.** Use the words in the box.

> One day, Saira found a chess board in her house. She was seven years old and she wanted to learn how to play, so she watched a video about the game. Then she joined a chess club and took part in a competition. She didn't win the competition, but she practised playing chess every day and she got much better. Now Saira is 20 years old and she's a famous chess player.

> when she was seven and 20 years old She wanted to learn how to play. She practised and got better.
>
> Saira home, chess club, competition chess, famous chess player

Who?	
When?	
Where?	
What?	
Why?	

B **Use your chart from the Unit 1 Writing Lesson to help you write a story about the pictures below.**

Who?	
When?	
Where?	
What?	
Why?	

A **Read.** Circle the best answers for you.

1. I like to challenge myself at school.

   a. Always   **b.** Sometimes   **c.** Never

2. I learn new things when I do something challenging.

   a. Always   **b.** Sometimes   **c.** Never

3. I feel scared when I do something challenging.

   a. Always   **b.** Sometimes   **c.** Never

4. When I challenge myself with something, I don't worry about getting it right.

   a. Always   **b.** Sometimes   **c.** Never

B **Why is it important to challenge yourself?** Tick the answers you think are true.

☐ It makes me happy.

☐ It helps me to learn new things.

☐ It makes people like me more.

☐ It helps me to feel less stressed.

☐ It helps me to feel good about myself.

C **Draw a picture of yourself doing something challenging.** Write why it is challenging.

In this picture, I _____

_____

_____ .

It's challenging because _____

_____

_____

_____

_____ .

Lesson 1 Vocabulary

A Circle the correct answer.

1. I want to make a cake. Can you get me some butter and *flour / pepper*, please?

2. Would you like a glass of milk and some *biscuits / salt*?

3. Do you always put salt and *sugar / pepper* on your food?

4. *Sugar / Pepper* tastes sweet, but it isn't good for you.

5. We can make *sugar / yoghurt* from milk.

6. Bees make *honey / salt*.

B Listen to Federico and Jay. Tick the food they've got. Put a cross for the food they haven't got. 🎧 TR: 2.1

C Choose one of the food words. Write about how often you eat it or them, and what you eat it or them with.

butter	biscuits	flour	honey
pepper	salt	sugar	yoghurt

I eat yoghurt every day. I usually eat it with honey or strawberries.

_____

_____

A **Circle the correct answer.**

1. I moved from Canada to *a / an /* (the) UK last year.

2. Johan gave Gisela *a / an / the* biscuit. *A / An / The* biscuit was cherry and chocolate.

3. I had *a / an / the* ice cream when I went to *a / an / the* zoo.

4. Look at *a / an / the* food! It looks delicious.

5. They want to buy *a / an / the* new car.

6. Jodie's father is *a / an / the* waiter.

7. This pancake is *a / an / the* biggest pancake I've ever eaten!

8. Do you want *a / an / the* apple?

B **Complete the conversations with *a, an* or *the*.**

1. **A:** Have you ever been to _____ pizza restaurant?

   B: Yes, I have been to _____ pizza restaurant next to _____ library.

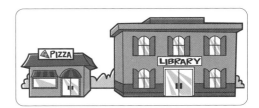

2. **A:** There's _____ famous pancake race in Olney every year.

   B: Yes, I know. My sister won _____ race last year!

3. **A:** Did you enjoy your holiday in _____ Netherlands?

   B: Yes, I did. _____ food there is delicious!

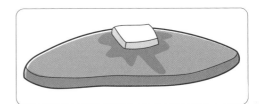

4. **A:** Is your cousin _____ teacher?

   B: No, he isn't. He's _____ student.

5. **A:** Would you like _____ sandwich for lunch?

   B: Yes, please. Can I have _____ apple as well, please?

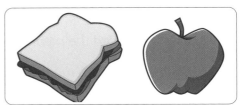

A **Scan the text.** Circle the best title. Then listen. 🎧 TR: 2.2

a. My Favourite Restaurant

b. The Restaurant with Robot Waiters

c. Robot Chefs

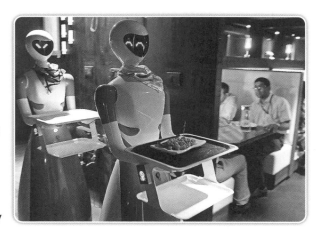

In Chennai, India, you can visit a very unusual place. Robot is a restaurant where some of the waiters aren't people – they're robots! It's the first robot restaurant in India. The restaurant opened in November 2017 and is very popular. Lots of people want to see the robots. There are 20 tables at Robot, and there are always **queues** of people waiting outside the restaurant every evening.

There are four robots at the restaurant. They are white and blue with red eyes. Each robot wears a blue, red, purple or pink scarf. Customers use tablets on their tables to **order** their food. The tablets send this information to the kitchen, where chefs prepare their **meal**. When the food is ready, the chefs give it to the robots. The robots then take the food to the tables. If someone stands in front of a robot, it stops and waits. When the robots arrive at the tables, human waiters take the food from the robots and give it to the customers. At the end of the meal, the robots take the dirty dishes back to the kitchen.

What do you think? Would you like to get your food from a robot waiter?

B **Read again.** Who does these things – R (robots) or H (humans)?

1. They wear scarves in different colours. _____

2. They order the food on tablets. _____

3. They prepare the food. _____

4. They take the food to the tables. _____

5. They give the food to the customers. _____

6. They take the dirty dishes to the kitchen. _____

C **Circle the correct answer.**

1. Thank you for the salad. It's *meal / delicious*.

2. The customer at the restaurant *ordered / prepared* a pizza and a glass of water.

3. Be careful with the *meal / knife*.

4. There was a long *meal / queue* outside the café.

5. Here's a *spoon / knife* for your soup.

6. I can't *prepare / order* dinner. We haven't got any food.

A Complete the sentences with *who, that* or *where*.

1. This is the house _____ my teacher lives.

2. The girl _____ made this cake is only ten years old.

3. The meal _____ you prepared is delicious.

4. This computer is the one _____ I bought last year.

5. Have you visited the farm _____ my brother works?

6. A waiter is a person _____ works in a café or restaurant.

7. Have you seen the book _____ I bought yesterday?

8. The children _____ are playing football are my cousins.

B **Awa is showing a friend a photo of her family.** Listen to the conversation. Match to form sentences. Complete the sentences with *who, that* or *where*. 🎧 TR: 2.3

1. Yoff is the town

2. Yande is the girl

3. Binta is the girl

4. Awa's uncle is the man

5. This is the camera

6. Awa's dad is the man

a. _____ is eating an ice cream.

b. _____ is next to the little boy.

c. _____ Awa's mum gave him.

d. _____ is wearing a big hat.

e. _____ is holding a camera.

f. _____ Awa's uncle's got a restaurant.

C Make each pair of sentences into one sentence with *who, that* or *where*.

1. He's a boy. He would like a pet snake.

   He's the boy _who / that would like a pet snake_____ .

2. It's a school. My dad teaches there.

   It's the school _____ .

3. They're singers. They won a singing competition last week.

   They're the singers _____ .

4. That's a park. I go running there every Saturday.

   That's the park _____ .

5. This is a bag. I bought it in Madrid.

   This is the bag _____ .

A **Complete the chart about a café review.** Use the information below.

The waiters were slow.	My burger tasted really nice.
The table was a bit dirty.	Yes! Not expensive.
Café Apple	You should try the ice cream.
It makes the best ice cream in town.	I liked the music.

Place and why famous?

_____

_____

What was good? What wasn't so good?

☺ _____

_____

☹ _____

_____

Recommend?

_____

_____

B **Use your chart from the Unit 2 Writing Lesson to help you write a review about a café or a restaurant.**

Last _____ visited the _____ on _____ . I was really looking forward to _____.

The _____ was _____ . _____

_____ . _____ , but _____

_____.

I would recommend the _____ . _____

_____.

VALUE
Eat healthily.

A **Match the descriptions (1–4) with the pictures (a–d).** Then tick the two healthy lunches.

1. Today, for my lunch, I've got some chicken with tomatoes and carrots. I've also got a small yoghurt and a bottle of water.

   Picture _____ ☐

2. I'm having a jam sandwich for lunch today, with an apple and a piece of cake.

   Picture _____ ☐

3. My lunch today is pizza. I've also got a chocolate biscuit and an orange.

   Picture _____ ☐

4. It's my favourite lunch today – rice with fish and broccoli. Then, I've got some strawberries and grapes and a glass of milk.

   Picture _____ ☐

a.

b.

c.

d.

B **Match to form sentences.**

1. You should eat five or six helpings   a. isn't good for you.
2. Too much fruit juice   b. with lots of salt in it.
3. Don't eat food   c. biscuits or cake.
4. Eat healthy snacks, like   d. of fruit or vegetables every day.
5. Don't eat lots of   e. apples or carrots.

C **Create your own healthy lunch. Include:**

one portion of pasta, potatoes, rice or bread   one portion of vegetables
one portion of milk, cheese or yoghurt   one portion of chicken, egg, fish or beans
one portion of fruit   one drink

For my lunch today, I've got _____

_____

_____

_____ .

A Read the sentences. Who says them? Write W (waiter) or C (customer).

1. Would you like any bread with that? _____

2. How was your food? _____

3. Could I have some chicken soup, please? _____

4. Can we have the bill, please? _____

5. I'd like some apple juice, please. _____

6. What would you like to drink? _____

B Complete the conversation with the sentences from Activity A.

Waiter: Hello! Welcome to Katya's Kitchen. Are you ready to order?

Priya: Yes, please. 1._____

Waiter: Yes, of course.

Ahmed: And I'd like a tomato salad, please.

Waiter: OK, that's great. 2._____

Priya: Yes, please.

Waiter: 3._____

Priya: I'll just have some water, please.

Ahmed: 4._____

Waiter: 5._____

Priya: It was delicious, thank you.

Waiter: Great! Would you like any dessert?

Ahmed: No, thank you. 6._____

Waiter: Of course. Here you are.

C Listen to the conversation at Katya's Kitchen. Complete the waiter's order pad. 🎧 TR: 2.4

Table 15	
Food	**Drinks**
pasta with tomato sauce	_____
_____	_____
small _____	

A Tick the plants and animals you can see in the video.

fish

octopus

sea urchins

sea turtle

seaweed

shark

B Circle the correct answer.

1. The Bajau people live in houses *above* / *under the water*.
2. They cook fish *in their kitchens* / *on their boats*.
3. Seaweed is very healthy and good for your *eyes* / *skin*.
4. The Bajau people *always* / *never* know what food they'll find.
5. They sometimes eat food from *shells* / *the supermarket*.

C **Imagine you are hunting for food in the sea.** Draw a picture and write about the food you find. Use the words in the box.

| catch | cook | find | hunt | look for |

In the sea, I _____

_____ .

I can also _____ ,

and some people _____

_____ .

A **Write the words that match each sentence and picture.** There are two words you don't need.

> biscuit   competition   flour   ~~honey~~   pepper   prize
>
> rider   stadium   sugar   winner   yoghurt

1. Bees make this. It's very sweet.

 honey

2. The person who comes first in a race.

 _____

3. There are big sports games in this place.

 _____

4. You can put this in your tea or coffee to make it sweet.

 _____

5. Some people have this with fruit for breakfast.

 _____

6. People have this as a snack. It isn't very healthy.

 _____

7. This person is on a horse.

 _____

8. You get this if you come first in a race.

 _____

9. You can make bread with this.

 _____

B **Listen to Teresa ask Ferdi some questions.** Circle the correct answer. TR: 2.5

1. Ferdi usually has toast with *honey / butter* for breakfast.
2. He *likes / doesn't like* coffee with sugar.
3. He *sometimes / never* eats biscuits between breakfast and lunch.
4. For lunch, he usually has a sandwich and then some *yoghurt / honey* with fruit.
5. He sometimes puts *pepper / salt* on his food.
6. He *often / never* does sports.

C **Complete the text with the verbs in parentheses.** Use the past simple or the past continuous.

My sister and I ¹· _____ (watch) TV when my brother ²· _____ (come) into our room. He ³· _____ (look for) our cat. We ⁴· _____ (open) the cupboard, but she wasn't there. Then we ⁵· _____ (look) under the bed, but she wasn't there. Then we ⁶· _____ (see) something at the window. It was our cat! She ⁷· _____ (sit) on a tree by the window, and she ⁸· _____ (hit) the window with her paw. My brother ⁹· _____ (put) a chair by the tree. He ¹⁰· _____ (stand) on the chair and ¹¹· _____ (climb) up the tree. Then he ¹²· _____ (carry) her down.

D **Complete the sentences with *a / an* or *the*.**

1. Is Anders from Belgium or _____ Netherlands?
2. Would you like _____ drink or _____ snack?
3. I read _____ really interesting book last week. _____ book was about chess.
4. Don't look at _____ sun! It's bad for your eyes.
5. It's _____ funniest film I've ever seen.
6. I want to be _____ actor when I leave school.
7. Have you ever seen _____ Empire State Building in New York?
8. There's _____ new teacher at our school. He's called Mr Shadid.

E **Complete the sentences using the correct relative pronoun – *who, where* or *that*.**

1. She's the teacher _____ works at our school.
2. It's the bag _____ I bought last week.
3. They're the students _____ play for the school football team.
4. This is the café _____ my aunt works.
5. That's the mountain _____ my brother climbed.
6. It's the house _____ my teacher lives.
7. This is the book _____ I'm reading at the moment.
8. That's the park _____ I play with my friends.

A Label the picture with the words from the box.

> audience   king   queen   stage   theatre

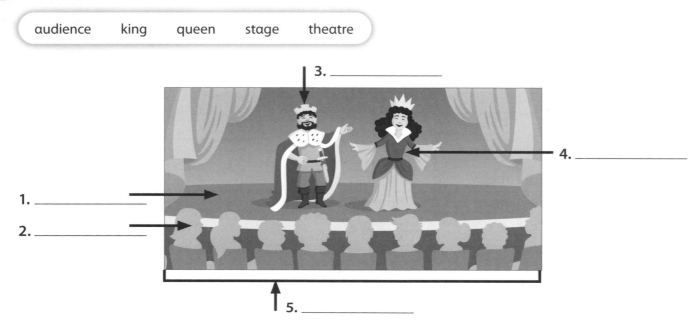

3. _____

4. _____

1. _____

2. _____

5. _____

B Circle the correct answer.

1. The girl on the *stage / audience* can sing very well, and she can *act / end* too!

2. A *fairy tale / queen* is a kind of *traditional / married* story.

3. I enjoyed the story, but it didn't *act / end* happily.

4. The woman met the man and then they *got married / ended*.

5. The *fairy tale / audience* loved the show.

C Listen to the conversation and complete the sentences. 🎧 TR: 3.1

1. The boy went to a _____ show.

2. The theatre was in the _____ .

3. The audience sat on _____ .

4. The show was about a beautiful _____ from the forest who meets a pirate.

5. They got _____ .

6. In the end, they lived on a _____ .

A **Put the words in order to make sentences.**

1. the / going / Is / circus / he / to / visit / ?

_____

2. aren't / show / watch / going / We / the / to / .

_____

3. to / story / read / going / I'm / this / .

_____

4. to / they / going / a / Are / song / sing / ?

_____

5. going / What / are / to / tomorrow / we / see / film / ?

_____

6. actor / to / going / be / She's / an / .

_____

B **Complete the conversation with *be going to* and the verbs in parentheses.**

A: What 1. _____are you going to do_____ (you / do) tomorrow?

B: Well, I won't be at school, of course, because it's the weekend! I 2. _____ (get up) late, and then my grandfather 3. _____ (take) me to the beach.

A: 4. _____ (you / swim) in the sea?

B: Probably. But my grandfather 5. _____ (not / go) in the water. It's too cold for him!

A: What about your brothers?

B: They 6. _____ (not / come) to the beach with us.
They 7. _____ (watch) a puppet show.

C **What are you going to do next week?** Write true sentences. Use the ideas in the box or your own ideas.

| do all my homework | eat some Vietnamese food | go to a puppet show | go to school |
| listen to some music | play football | play the flute | watch TV |

Next week, I'm going to _____

_____

_____ .

I'm not going to _____

_____

_____ .

A **Look at the photo and the title.** Guess. What is 'Behind the Door'? Then listen.

    a. a street theatre festival   **b.** a fairy tale   **c.** a circus show

Behind the Door 🎧 TR: 3.2

It's a warm evening in July, and I'm in Prague in the Czech Republic. There are lots of people here, and we're all watching some diggers – big machines that dig holes. But they aren't digging holes today. They're performing a **ballet**. Now the dancing has finished and I'm watching a juggler. She's throwing fire sticks high up into the air. Suddenly she falls onto the ground. Is she going to drop the fire sticks? No, she catches them all, and the audience laughs and claps loudly.

Every July, for five days, street performers from all around the world come to Prague to take part in Behind the Door – the Prague Street Theatre Festival. There are more than forty different shows at the festival, including huge puppets, clowns, acrobats, musicians and people who walk on **stilts**. Perhaps you'd prefer to watch a film? You can visit a yurt – a traditional tent – and watch Piotr and Jacek. Piotr is an actor and Jacek is a musician. Together, they perform a film story with **mime**, music and sounds but no words.

Would you like to take part in a street theatre festival? What would your show be about?

B **Read the text.** Answer the questions.

1. What are the diggers doing?

    _____

2. Do the people in the audience like the juggler's performance? How do you know?

    _____

3. How long is the festival?

    _____

4. Where can you watch a film story with no words?

    _____

C **Match the words in the box with the pictures (1–4).** There are two words you don't need.

    acrobatics   ballet   life   mime   stilts   value

1. _____   **2.** _____   **3.** _____   **4.** _____

A **Match the sentences (1–6) with the predictions (a–f).**

1. There aren't any clouds in the sky.
2. She's the best singer in the competition.
3. She's got eggs, sugar, flour and butter.
4. The actors are on the stage.
5. I'm scared of clowns.
6. It's eight o'clock and we haven't left home yet.

a. She's going to make a cake.
b. The show is going to start soon.
c. I'm not going to enjoy the circus.
d. We're going to be late for school.
e. It isn't going to rain.
f. She's going to win the prize.

B **Listen to the conversation.** Complete the predictions (1–4) with *be going to* and the phrases from the box. TR: 3.3

be late   be very tired tomorrow   love the show   not be warm enough

1. They _____ .
2. A T-shirt _____ .
3. The boy _____ .
4. The girl _____ .

C **Look at the pictures.** Make predictions using *be going to* and the words in the box. Then draw your own picture and write a prediction.

eat the sandwich   fall off the stage   lose the game   win the game

1. The dancer _____ .

0:08 LINDTHORN SCHOOL 0 BLACKFIELD SCHOOL 7

2. Blackfield School _____ .
3. Lindthorn School _____ .

4. The cat _____ .

5. _____ .

A Complete the chart about a script. Use the information below.

at the circus	They have to wait to get in.
There aren't many people so they can get in anyway.	Grandad
They realise their tickets are wrong.	Sally

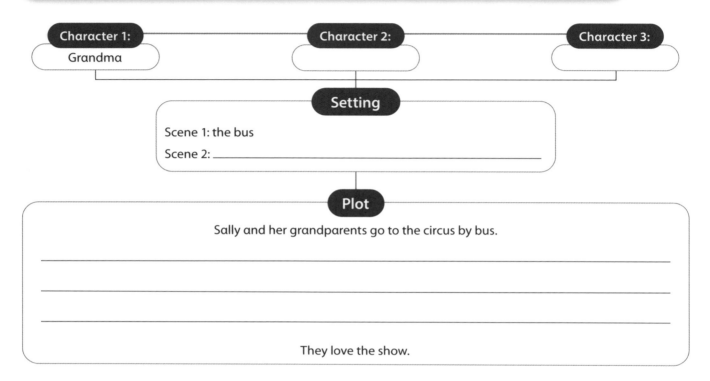

Character 1: Grandma   **Character 2:**   **Character 3:**

Setting

Scene 1: the bus

Scene 2: _____

Plot

Sally and her grandparents go to the circus by bus.

_____

_____

_____

They love the show.

B Use your chart from the Unit 3 Writing Lesson to help you write a script.

Scene 1: _____

_____ : _____

_____ : _____

_____ : _____

_____ : _____

_____ : _____

_____ : _____

_____ : _____

VALUE

Work together.

A **Look at the pictures.** Tick the pictures that show people working together. Put a cross when they aren't working together.

1.  ☐

2.  ☐

3.  ☐

4.  ☐

5. ☐

6.  ☐

B **Read the text and answer the questions.**

Last week my friends and I worked together to write a show about our favourite festival. First, we thought about different festivals from around the world. We chose the King's Day Festival from the Netherlands. It isn't my favourite festival, but it was the best one for our group. Ricardo is good at making things, so he made some amazing costumes. Theo and I drew a poster for the show. Theo wrote the script because he loves writing. Ricardo and I acted in the show. It was great!

1. Did the students work together? _____

2. Why did they choose this festival? _____

3. Why did Ricardo make the costumes? _____

4. Why did Theo write the script? _____

5. Was the show good or bad? _____

C **Think about when you work in a group.** Take the quiz. Do you ...

listen to other people in the group?	Always	Sometimes	Never
ask other people for their ideas?	Always	Sometimes	Never
find out what other people like doing?	Always	Sometimes	Never
make sure that everyone in the group is happy?	Always	Sometimes	Never

Score 3 points for every 'always' answer.
Score 2 points for every 'sometimes' answer.
Score 1 point for every 'never' answer.

If your score is 10–12 points
You are great at working in a group!

If your score is 7–9 points
You are good at working with other people, but sometimes you prefer to work on your own.

If your score is 4–6 points
You probably prefer working on your own. That's OK, but think about other people as well.

4 How Is It Made?

A **Look at the photos.** Complete the labels.

1.

m _ _ _ _ tin

2.

c _ _ _ _ _ _ _ _
box

3.

w _ _ _ _ _ spoon

4.

g _ _ _ _ jar

B **Circle the correct answer.**

How to Make Scrambled Eggs

Put two eggs in a bowl. [1.] *Pour / Cool* 200 millilitres of milk onto the eggs. Add some salt and pepper and [2.] *mix / burn* them all together. Then [3.] *pour / heat* some butter in a pan. Add the eggs and milk to the pan and cook for one minute. Be careful – the mixture cooks very quickly, so make sure it doesn't [4.] *cool / burn*!

C **Listen and complete the recipe for muffins.** 🎧 TR: 4.1

1. _____ together some flour, butter and sugar with a _____ _____ .

2. Add _____ eggs and some milk.

3. _____ the mixture into a _____ _____ .

4. Cook the mixture in the oven for _____ minutes.

5. Take the tin out of the oven and wait for the muffins to _____ .

A Match to make present simple passive sentences.

1. Polish	are used	at cinemas.
2. Halwa	are taught	in China.
3. Chopsticks	is grown	in schools.
4. Coffee	is made	in Brazil.
5. Films	is spoken	in Bahrain.
6. Students	are shown	in Poland.

B Listen and complete the notes about chocolate with the verbs from the box. Use the present simple passive form. TR: 4.2

> cut (x2)   dry   grow   heat   keep   mix   send   take (x2)

How Chocolate Is Made

Chocolate comes from cocoa pods, which 1. _____

on trees. The cocoa pods 2. _____ open, and the

cocoa beans 3. _____ out. Then the beans

4. _____ in big plastic pots for a week or longer.

After that, they 5. _____ in the sun. Then they

6. _____ to factories.

At the factories, the beans 7. _____ and the shells

8. _____ off. The beans 9. _____ into very

small pieces. The cocoa 10. _____ with sugar, milk

and oil to make delicious chocolate.

C Choose a country from the box or another country you know about. Write three sentences about the country. Use the present simple passive form of the verbs in the other box.

> Australia   Brazil   China   Egypt   France

> eat   grow   speak

French is spoken in France.

_____

_____

_____

A **Scan the text.** Circle the best description of the text. Then listen.

a. The text describes how to drive a Ferrari.

b. The text describes a Formula 1 race.

c. The text describes how Ferraris are made.

The Ferrari Factory 🎧 TR: 4.3

Ferrari is one of the most famous **brands** of sports car in the world. Its yellow and black 'prancing horse' logo is known around the world, and Ferrari has the **record** for the most wins in Formula 1 competitions. So where are these amazing sports cars made? They all come from the Ferrari factory in their home country – Italy.

The Ferrari factory is in the town of Maranello. The factory is a huge place – as big as almost 20 large football pitches – with 45 different buildings. It takes about three weeks to **manufacture** a Ferrari. Different parts of the car are put together in different buildings. Then the car is tested carefully. For the final and most important test, the car is driven around a special racetrack at the factory.

Ferrari doesn't make many cars. Toyota, for example, makes millions of cars every year, but Ferrari only makes 7,000 cars a year. Would you like to buy a Ferrari? You have to be rich, and you have to wait! The cheapest new Ferrari costs around €240,000, and people usually have to wait for two years before their Ferrari is **delivered**!

B **Read again.** Write T (true) or F (false).

1. Ferrari has won a lot of Formula 1 competitions. _____

2. Some Ferraris are made in Italy and some are made in other countries. _____

3. The Ferrari factory in Maranello is much bigger than 50 football pitches. _____

4. Someone drives Ferraris around a racetrack at the factory to test them. _____

5. Toyota doesn't make as many cars as Ferrari. _____

6. You usually can't get a new Ferrari very quickly. _____

C **Match the words (1–7) with the definitions (a–g).**

1. brand

2. deliver

3. manufacture

4. fabric

5. assembly line

6. dye

7. record

a. the way people work in a factory

b. cloth used for making clothes

c. a type of product made by one company

d. the best result

e. take something to someone

f. change the colour of something

g. make

A Make present simple passive questions with the words. Then match them with the answers (a–f).

1. where / Ferraris / manufacture?
   <u>Where are Ferraris manufactured?</u>

2. who / students / teach / by?
   _____

3. what / cupcakes / make / from?
   _____

4. where / coffee / grow?
   _____

5. who / photographs / take / by?
   _____

6. where / medicine / sell?
   _____

a. flour, butter, sugar and eggs   _____
b. in a factory in Italy   <u>1</u>
c. in Africa, Asia and South America   _____

d. at a pharmacy or chemist's   _____
e. photographers   _____
f. teachers   _____

B Make these active sentences and questions into passive sentences and questions.

1. They don't grow tea in France. <u>Tea isn't grown in France.</u>

2. They don't speak German in Australia. _____

3. Where do they make Audi cars? _____

4. What kind of food do they eat in your country? _____

5. They don't sell Ferraris in the supermarket. _____

6. Who treats sick people? _____

C Think of present simple passive questions for these answers. Use the words in the box or your own ideas.

China   pancakes   ~~pasta~~   plane   Spanish   sushi

1. <u>Where is pasta eaten?</u>   in Italy

2. _____   in Japan

3. _____   in Mexico

4. _____   flour, eggs and milk

5. _____   tea

6. _____   a pilot

A **Complete the chart about an invention.** Use the information below.

> Salt in the water makes energy and passes through the wires to turn on the light bulb.
>
> a lamp that works with salt water   It produces light and charges mobile phone batteries.
>
> designer Aisa Mijeno   a lightbulb, wires, a handle, a water container

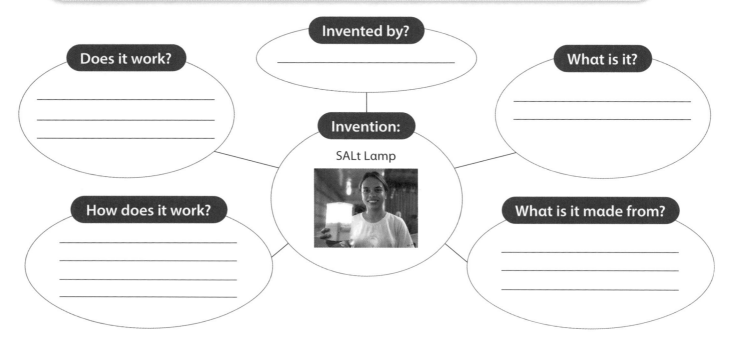

Invented by? _____

Does it work? _____

What is it? _____

Invention:
SALt Lamp

How does it work? _____

What is it made from? _____

B **Use your chart from the Unit 4 Writing Lesson to help you write a factfile about an invention.**

Name of Invention: _____

Inventor(s)?

• _____

What is it?

• _____

What is it made from?

• _____

How does it work?

• _____

Does it work?

• _____

Think about where things come from.

A **Match the descriptions (1–5) with the objects (a–e).**

1. It's made of wood. I keep it in my backpack. _____
2. It's made of glass. It's part of a house. _____
3. It's made of paper. You read it every day. _____
4. It's made of plastic. Food is kept in it. _____
5. It's made of plastic. Recycling is put in it. _____

a.

b.

c.

d.

e.

B **Do you know where these things are from?** Circle the correct answer.

1. Kimonos are worn in *France / Japan*.
2. Tacos are eaten in *Russia / Mexico*.
3. Euros are used as money in parts of *Asia / Europe*.
4. Bananas can be grown in *Ecuador / Scotland*.
5. The fabric of jeans is made *by machines / in kitchens*.

Where are kimonos worn?

Where are tacos eaten?

A Write the correct times for these clocks.

1.

_____

2.

_____

3.

_____

4.

_____

5.

_____

6.

_____

B Complete the conversation with the phrases from the box.

| Are you free   Do you want to   I'll see you   Sorry   Why don't we |

Li Na: 1. _____ go to the beach tomorrow morning?

Zhang Min: 2. _____ , I'm busy tomorrow. I'm visiting my grandparents.

Li Na: Oh, OK. 3. _____ on Sunday?

Zhang Min: Yes, I am.

Li Na: Great! 4. _____ meet at the bus station?

Zhang Min: OK. What time?

Li Na: There's a bus to the beach at two thirty, so how about quarter past two?

Zhang Min: Great idea! 5. _____ at the bus station then.

C Listen to Mason and Jack. Then complete the text below. 🎧 TR: 4.4

Jack's got a 1. p_____ l_____ on Thursday afternoon. He's playing in a football match on

2. F_____ a_____ . He's going to Mason's house on 3. S_____ m_____ at

4. t_____ o_____ . They're going to 5. w_____ to the sports centre. At the sports

centre, they're going to play 6. b_____ .

Shadow Puppet Shows

A **Listen and tick the information that is mentioned.** 🎧 TR: 4.5

- [ ] what the most famous show is about
- [ ] what the puppets are made of
- [ ] how the puppeteers learn their job
- [ ] what the puppeteers do
- [ ] when the shadow puppet show started in Indonesia
- [ ] the type of characters in a shadow puppet show
- [ ] why the puppeteers are amazing
- [ ] how the musicians work with the puppeteers

B **Listen again.** Write T (true) or F (false). Then correct the false sentences. 🎧 TR: 4.5

1. In *Wayang Kulit, wayang* means puppet and *kulit* means leather. _____

2. The screen in a *Wayang Kulit* show is made from a white sheet. _____

3. All the *Wayang Kulit* puppets are the same size. _____

4. In each *Wayang Kulit* show there are many puppeteers. _____

5. The puppeteer uses three sticks to move each puppet. _____

6. The puppeteer tells the musicians when to change the music. _____

C **Read the sentences about the *Shadow Puppet Shows*.** Then circle the best definition (a or b) for the phrases in bold.

1. It is **a kind of** shadow puppet show called *Wayang Kulit*.

   a. similar to   **b.** a type of

2. For each show, there is **only one** puppeteer.

   a. a big number   **b.** a small number

3. One of the most amazing things about the *Wayang Kulit* is that a show can last all night, sometimes **up to ten hours**!

   a. ten hours or less   **b.** more than ten hours

D **Complete the sentences about the text.**

1. I was interested to learn that _____.

2. To me, it was amazing that _____.

3. I would like to ask a puppeteer this question: '_____?'

A **Complete the words.**

Across

1. Actors do this
2. A traditional story
5. Sometimes the most important man in a country
6. Actors stand on this

Down

1. The people who watch a play or show
3. Sometimes the most important woman in a country
4. You go to this place to watch plays and shows

B **Circle the correct answer.**

1. Please put the jam mixture in the fridge to *heat / cool*.

2. It's better to keep jam in a *glass / metal* jar.

3. Watch the biscuits carefully! They might *burn / mix*.

4. Can you *pour / heat* some water into a glass for me, please?

5. This biscuit *looks like / likes* a flower.

6. You can *mix / heat* the oil and sugar with a *wooden / cardboard* spoon.

C Listen to the conversation and complete the sentences. Use *be going to* with the correct phrase from the box. 🎧 TR: 4.6

| be in a big tent | ~~go to the circus~~ | meet his friends |
| (not) go swimming | (not) go with her | play badminton |

1. The girl _____is going to go to the circus_____ with her cousins.
2. The circus _____ in the town square.
3. Her brother _____ .
4. He _____ at the sports centre.
5. They _____ in the new pool.
6. They _____ at the sports centre.

D Write predictions about these situations with *be going to*. Use the words in the box.

| be angry | be late | be very happy | drop something | ~~feel sick~~ | get wet |

1. She's eaten ten biscuits.

   She 's going to feel sick. _____

2. I've made a delicious cake for my aunt.

   She _____

3. I've lost my brother's favourite T-shirt.

   He _____

4. It's raining, and we haven't got an umbrella.

   We _____

5. The bus is very slow today.

   We _____

6. I'm carrying four plates and five glasses.

   I _____

5 Awesome Animals

A Match the words (1–8) with the definitions (a–h).

1. ocean _____
2. artist _____
3. creature _____
4. protect _____
5. extinct _____
6. disappear _____
7. damage _____
8. environment _____

a. an animal
b. the sea
c. to go away
d. to take care of something
e. to hurt something
f. the world around us
g. no longer exists
h. a person who draws, paints or designs things

B Listen to the podcast about the giant ibis. Circle the correct answer (a or b). 🎧 TR: 5.1

1. The giant Ibis lives in _____.
   a. the sea
   b. rivers and wetlands
2. It lives in _____.
   a. Cambodia
   b. Canada
3. There are only _____.
   a. two hundred giant ibises left
   b. one hundred giant ibises left
4. The giant ibis is in danger because _____.
   a. people are cutting down forests
   b. it's a very big bird
5. The giant ibis is also in danger because its environment is becoming _____.
   a. wetter
   b. drier

A giant ibis in Tmatboey, Cambodia

C Choose a creature you think we need to protect. Answer the questions.

1. What's the creature called? _____

2. Where does it live? _____

3. Why do we need to protect it? _____

4. What can we do to protect it? _____

A **Look at these first conditional sentences.** Circle the present simple verbs and underline the future verbs.

1. If more people see Asher Jay's bottles, maybe they won't throw plastic into the sea.
2. If we don't protect creatures in danger, they won't be here in the future.
3. The giant ibis won't survive if people cut down the forests.
4. We'll have a picnic on the beach tomorrow if the weather is good.
5. If I miss the bus, I won't arrive at school on time.
6. He'll get good grades at school if he studies hard.

B **Circle the correct answers.**

1. If people *cut / will cut* down trees and forests, it *is / will be* difficult for the giant ibis to survive.
2. There *isn't / won't be* any more giant ibises in the future if people *will collect / collect* their eggs.
3. If we *will throw / throw* plastic into the sea, we *damage / will damage* the environment.
4. More people *know / will know* about creatures in danger if artists *draw / will draw* pictures of them.
5. If we *don't protect / won't protect* creatures in danger, they *will disappear / disappear*.

C **Complete the first conditional sentences with your own ideas.**

1. Creatures in danger will die if _____.
2. If people throw plastic into the sea, _____.
3. We'll damage the environment if _____.
4. If it's sunny tomorrow, _____.
5. I'll be very tired tomorrow if _____.
6. If you study hard, _____.

A green sea turtle near Sipadan Island, Malaysia

A **Look at the photo and read the text.** Write *Yes* or *No*. Then listen.

1. Are pangolins in danger? _____

2. Is it easy to see them during the day? _____

3. Is anyone trying to help protect them? _____

Good News for Pangolins! 🎧 TR: 5.2

Have you ever heard of a pangolin? It's a quiet creature about the same size as a cat. Pangolins live in Asia and southern Africa. They have long tails and are covered in **scales** – like tiny dinosaurs! Their long tongues are good for catching insects to eat. Some types of pangolins use their tails to help them climb trees and hang from branches.

Pangolins are nocturnal, which means they sleep during the day and come out at night. If they're frightened, they **roll** up into a ball, so that bigger animals like lions or tigers can't see them. If the pangolin has babies, it rolls around them so that the babies are protected.

A pangolin

The sad news is that people catch pangolins for their meat, and sometimes they are used for medicine. However, there's more information about these animals now and about the dangers they face. A lot of people are worried about pangolins and are interested in protecting them for the future. There's even a new **law** to stop people from catching and selling pangolins. So the good news for pangolins is that the people who catch them are now in **trouble**.

B **Read again.** Answer the questions.

1. Where do pangolins live?

   _____

2. What do some types of pangolins use their tails for?

   _____

3. How do they protect their babies?

   _____

4. Why do people catch pangolins?

   _____

5. What's the good news for pangolins?

   _____

C **Complete the sentences.**

   law   roll   scales   trouble

1. If we damage the environment, people and creatures will be in _____ .

2. Some creatures like pangolins are covered in _____ to protect their bodies.

3. Something round, like a ball, will _____ along the ground.

4. If something's a _____ , you must do what it says.

A Listen to the podcast and match the people (1–5) with the things they want to do (a–e). 🎧 TR: 5.3

1. Anisha _____
2. Santiago _____
3. Viktor _____
4. Harry _____
5. Amy _____

a. fly to the moon
b. fly across the sea to look for green sea turtles
c. go to India to see tigers
d. visit his grandma in Spain
e. fly to the top of a mountain

A Bengal tiger in a forest

B Complete the conditional sentences with the correct form of the verbs in parentheses.

1. If you _____ (find) a pangolin near your school, what _____ you _____ (do)?
2. If I _____ (have) a tail, I _____ (use) it to help me climb trees.
3. If fish _____ (not / have) tails, they _____ (not / be able to) swim.
4. If you _____ (see) a huge spider on your desk, how _____ you _____ (feel)?
5. Where _____ you _____ (fly) if you _____ (have) wings?

C Complete the second conditional sentences with your own ideas.

1. If I had wings, I _____.

2. If more people knew about pangolins, they _____.

3. If there were no cars in the world, we _____.

4. If our teacher wasn't at school today, we _____.

5. If I saw a tiger, I _____.

A **Complete the chart for a factfile about squirrels.** Use the information below.

all over the world except Australia and Antarctica   nuts, fruit, insects, eggs

about 25 cm and 500 grams (Eastern grey squirrel)   run up to 20 mph

between 2–24 years (depending on the species)   front teeth never stop growing

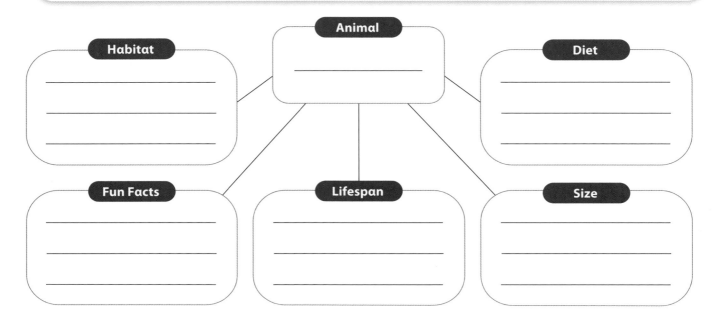

B **Use your chart from the Unit 5 Writing Lesson to help you write a factfile.**

Animal Factfile: _____

Habitat
* _____

Diet
* _____

Size
* _____

Lifespan
* _____

Fun Facts
* _____
_____
_____
_____

VALUE

Use your imagination.

A **Read.** Circle the best answers for you.

1. If I could fly, I'd fly over …

a.

b.

c.

2. If I could be a big animal, I'd be a / an …

a.

b.

c.

3. If animals could speak, I'd like to talk to a …

a.

b.

c.

4. If I were an insect, I'd be a / an …

a.

b.

c.

B **When and why do you use your imagination?** Tick the answers that are true for you.

I use my imagination …

- [ ] when I play games.
- [ ] when I'm with my friends.
- [ ] to tell a story.
- [ ] to solve a problem.
- [ ] when I'm drawing a picture.

C **When was the last time you used your imagination?** Draw a picture of what happened. Write how your imagination helped you.

In this picture, I _____

_____

_____ .

My imagination helped me because _____

_____

_____ .

6 Working Outdoors

Lesson 1 Vocabulary

A **Match to form correct sentences.**

1. If you are a lifeguard, you _____

2. A mountain guide _____

3. A mechanic is someone who _____

4. Marine biologists _____

5. A person who takes photos for news stories _____

6. A gardener _____

a. has to look after plants and flowers.

b. is a photojournalist.

c. make sure that people on the beach are safe.

d. leads walkers and climbers on a mountain.

e. study creatures that live in the sea.

f. is good at fixing cars.

B **Listen to the podcast and write the jobs.** You don't need two of the jobs. 🎧 TR: 6.1

| gardener | lifeguard | marine biologist | mechanic |
| mountain guide | painter | photojournalist | tennis coach |

1. Marta: _____

2. Bill: _____

3. Isabella: _____

4. Olaf: _____

5. Miki: _____

6. Jordi: _____

C **Choose two jobs you would like to do and two you would not like to do.** Give your reasons.

I would like to be a lifeguard because I like the sea.

I wouldn't like to be a painter because I'd get tired.

_____

_____

_____

_____

_____

_____

A Circle the correct answer.

1. *Anyone / No one* lives on the moon.

2. A gardener is *someone / something* who looks after plants and flowers.

3. Do you have *anything / nothing* in your bag?

4. We should do *everyone / everything* we can to look after our planet.

5. The mountain guide led *everyone / anyone* safely down the path.

6. The marine biologist saw *something / anything* interesting under the water.

B Complete the sentences. Use indefinite pronouns.

1. A tennis coach is _____ who shows people how to play tennis.

2. A lifeguard makes sure that _____ is in danger on the beach or in the water.

3. If you need to fix _____ , you should ask a mechanic to help you.

4. We want to climb this mountain, but we don't know the way. Does _____ know a good mountain guide?

5. Is there _____ we can get ice cream?

6. Have you got _____ to eat? I'm really hungry.

C Write sentences. Use the words and your own ideas.

1. nothing / TV

   There's nothing interesting on TV this evening. _____

2. someone / my lunch

   _____

3. no one / homework

   _____

4. everyone / the environment

   _____

5. anything / cupboard?

   _____

6. anyone / beach?

   _____

A **Scan the text.** What two cool jobs does the text talk about? Then listen. 🎧 TR: 6.2

_____

Two Cool Jobs!

If you like ice cream, a job as an ice cream taster would be a very good job for you – as long as you could taste 32 different kinds of ice cream before lunch! Ice cream tasters check that ice cream is delicious and safe for everyone to eat. Everything they wear must be clean, and they have to make sure that nothing falls into the ice cream while they're tasting it.

This job isn't only about eating ice cream. You need some **skills** too. To become an ice cream taster, you'll have to study food science or food technology. You also need to be good at writing because you'll need to write ice cream reviews.

Ice-cream tasters at work in the company's laboratory

If you enjoy being outdoors all day, you might enjoy being a park ranger. Park rangers look after the environment by protecting rivers, lakes and forests. They also try to make sure no one's in danger when they visit a park. Also, they let everyone know if there's a problem such as a fire in the park.

Park rangers need certain skills too. They must be good at teaching and helping people. It's also helpful to be interested in plants and flowers. Park rangers work hard – often at weekends and during the holidays – but they're usually outdoors in a beautiful place.

B **Read again.** Complete the table.

	Indoors or outdoors?	Skills needed?	Things you'd like about the job?	Things you wouldn't like about the job?
Ice cream taster				
Park ranger				

C **Match the words (1–5) with the definitions (a–e).**

1. skills _____
2. ranger _____
3. mural _____
4. passionate _____
5. wonder _____

a. to think and want to know about something
b. a painting on a wall
c. useful things you can do
d. someone who takes care of forests, parks, etc.
e. having strong feelings

A Circle the correct answer (a, b or c).

1. Rhino keepers look after rhinos, _____ ?

   a. aren't they   b. don't they   c. do they

2. She paints fantastic murals, _____ ?

   a. doesn't she   b. does she   c. didn't she

3. He's an ice-cream taster, _____ ?

   a. is he   b. doesn't he   c. isn't he

4. We're not going swimming tomorrow, _____ ?

   a. are we   b. don't we   c. do we

5. I'm coming to your house tonight, _____ ?

   a. aren't you   b. am I   c. aren't I

6. He's got a bike, _____ ?

   a. doesn't he   b. hasn't he   c. isn't he

B Listen to the interview. Complete the question tags. Then write the correct answers. 🎧 TR: 6.3

1. Alice enjoys her job, _____ ? _____ .

2. Alice looked after sheep and lambs when she was little, _____ ? _____ .

3. If you're a vet, you sometimes have to get up in the middle of the night, _____ ?

   _____ .

4. It's not very hard to become a vet, _____ ? _____ .

5. Alice is very happy, _____ ? _____ .

C Choose two jobs from the box. Write two sentences with question tags for a person who does each job.

| ice-cream taster   mural painter   park ranger   vet   wildlife keeper |

Job: **Job:**

_____   _____

1. _____ , _____ ?   1. _____ , _____ ?
2. _____ , _____ ?   2. _____ , _____ ?

A Complete the chart for an informational text about a bridge painter's job. Use the information below.

learn painting skills

uses climbing equipment

works outdoors and high up

someone who knows about bridges, metals and paint

get training and experience

first cleans old paint, then paints

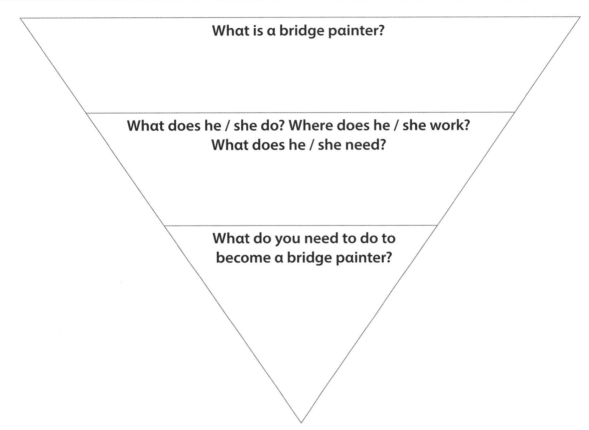

What is a bridge painter?

What does he / she do? Where does he / she work?
What does he / she need?

What do you need to do to
become a bridge painter?

B Use your chart from the Unit 6 Writing Lesson to help you write an informational text.

A(n) _____ Job

_____ . They know a lot about

_____ . They work _____

_____ .

If you want to become a(n) _____ ,

you have to _____ . You also need to _____

_____ .

VALUE
Stay safe.

A **Read.** Tick the sentences that tell us how you can stay safe. Put a cross for the unsafe actions.

☐ 1. Check that there's a lifeguard on the beach before you go swimming.

☐ 2. Ask a mountain guide to help you when you are walking in the mountains.

☐ 3. If you see a rattlesnake, get close to it and take a photo.

☐ 4. If you go out alone, tell someone where you're going.

☐ 5. Give people you don't know your phone number.

☐ 6. Don't wear a helmet when you ride your bike.

☐ 7. Look carefully to check that there are no cars before you walk across a road.

B **Look at the picture and circle three examples that show people who are not staying safe.** Then write a sentence about each problem.

_____

_____

_____

C **Think of some things you do to stay safe.** Write four sentences about them.

I never go swimming alone.

_____

_____

_____

_____

A Tick the expressions you can use for giving advice.

1. It's a good idea to ...   [   ]   7. Why don't you ...?   [   ]

2. Maro had an idea.   [   ]   8. You might try ...   [   ]

3. Don't forget to ...   [   ]   9. Mr Suzuki tried to ...   [   ]

4. Kenji tries to ...   [   ]   10. If I were you, I'd ...   [   ]

5. You should ...   [   ]   11. That would be great!   [   ]

6. Can we put up a poster?   [   ]

B **Kenji and Maro are asking for advice about starting a recycling club.** Listen and complete the conversation with the expressions from Activity A. 🎧 TR: 6.4

Kenji: Hello, Mr Suzuki. Maro and I really want to do something to help the environment. We'd like to start a recycling club at school.

Mr Suzuki: Oh, that would be great!

Maro: Can you give us any advice?

Mr Suzuki: Well, _____ start by having a meeting. Then you can decide what you want to do and how you're going to do it. _____ put up a poster so that a lot of people know about the meeting.

Kenji: That's a great idea. Where should we put the poster?

Mr Suzuki: _____ make lots of posters? Then you can put them up all around the school.

Maro: What else should we do?

Mr Suzuki: _____ putting a big recycling bin for plastic in each classroom. Then students can throw plastic rubbish into the bins so that it can be recycled! _____ also make signs for the recycling bins, so that people know what they're for.

Kenji: We could have recycling bins for paper too.

Mr Suzuki: Yes, of course. Good idea. _____ make it fun. For example, you could have a competition to see which class can make the best sculpture out of plastic rubbish.

Maro: Great idea! Thanks for the advice, Mr Suzuki.

Mr Suzuki: No problem. Good luck!

A **Remember the video.** Match the animals in the box with the photos.

Mola mola fish   pelagic sea cucumber   silky shark   swordfish

1.
_____

3.
_____

2.
_____

4.
_____

B **Circle the correct answer.**

1. The submarine *went* / *didn't go* all the way to the Pacific Ocean floor.
2. The lights on the submarine *were* / *weren't* very bright.
3. Jess Cramp was working with *three* / *two* other women.
4. Jess and her team work hard to protect *submarines* / *marine life*.

C **Imagine you are in a submarine in the Galapagos Islands.** Describe your journey.

Where are you going?

We're travelling in a submarine to the bottom of the Pacific Ocean.
_____

What can you see?
_____
_____

How do you feel?
_____
_____

A **Complete the text with the words from the box.**

> artist   creatures   damage   disappearing
>
> environment   extinct   marine   protect

My friend and I are going to join a club for ¹· _____ animals. It's a club that wants to

²· _____ all the ³· _____ that live in the sea. The first meeting

is at four o'clock on Tuesday. We're going to make sculptures out of plastic rubbish.

A(n) ⁴· _____ is going to help us. We hope our work will make people think more

about the ⁵· _____ and how the rubbish we create can ⁶· _____ sea

life. If we want to stop more sea animals from ⁷· _____ and becoming

⁸· _____, we need to stop throwing plastic into the sea.

B **Match the jobs (1–8) with the descriptions (a–h).**

1. tennis coach _____
2. photojournalist _____
3. painter _____
4. lifeguard _____
5. mechanic _____
6. gardener _____
7. marine biologist _____
8. mountain guide _____

a. someone who helps make houses, buildings and other places look nice or paints pictures
b. someone who fixes things like cars and motorcycles
c. someone who leads people up and down mountains
d. someone who teaches people how to play tennis
e. someone who takes photos for news stories
f. someone who keeps people safe while swimming
g. someone who studies fish and other marine creatures
h. someone who grows plants and flowers

C **Listen to the interview about a job. Circle the correct answer.** 🎧 TR: 6.5

1. Amy is a *swimming instructor / lifeguard*.
2. When she was small, she lived near *the sea / a lake*.
3. She taught her *little sister / grandmother* to swim.
4. Her grandmother's *friend / little sister* wants to learn to swim.
5. Amy thinks it's *sometimes / never* too late to learn to swim.
6. When people swim for the first time, they might be *happy / scared*.

D **Match to form correct sentences.**

1. If I get up early, ___
2. If I got up early, ___
3. If we recycle our plastic, ___
4. If we recycled our plastic, ___
5. If we exercise more, ___
6. If we exercised more, ___
7. If we don't try to look after animals that are in danger, ___
8. If we didn't try to look after animals that are in danger, ___

a. it would be better for the environment.
b. they would disappear.
c. they'll disappear.
d. we would get stronger.
e. I'll arrive at school on time.
f. it'll be better for the environment.
g. we'll get stronger.
h. I would arrive at school on time.

E **Add question tags to these statements.** Then write the answers.

1. Mechanics can repair cars, _____ ?

   _____ .

2. Coaltan Tanner is the youngest person to climb Mount Kilimanjaro, _____ ?

   _____ .

3. Marine biologists don't study marine creatures, _____ ?

   _____ .

4. Camera traps don't hurt the animals, _____ ?

   _____ .

5. Pangolins use their tails to hang from branches, _____ ?

   _____ .

6. It isn't difficult to set an alarm on a mobile phone, _____ ?

   _____ .

7 At the Museum

A **Where did Paulo and Oscar see each of these things at the museum?** Listen and write the correct letter in each box. There is one example. 🎧 TR: 7.1

1.
   mural d

2.
   teeth ☐

3.
   book ☐

4.
   sandwiches ☐

5.
   guitar ☐

6.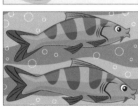
   fish ☐

a.

b.

c.

d.

e.

f.

g.

h.

A **Match the direct speech (1–8) with the reported speech (a–h).**

1. Paulo: The exhibition is fascinating. _____
2. Paulo: The exhibition was fascinating. _____
3. Oscar: We entered a competition. _____
4. Oscar: We're going to enter a competition. _____
5. Paulo: I didn't go to the café. _____
6. Paulo: I'm not going to go to the café. _____
7. Oscar: We went back to the museum. _____
8. Oscar: We'll go back to the museum. _____

a. Oscar said they had gone back to the museum.
b. Paulo said he wasn't going to go to the café.
c. Oscar said they would go back to the museum.
d. Oscar said they had entered a competition.
e. Paulo said that the exhibition was fascinating.
f. Paulo said he hadn't gone to the café.
g. Oscar said they were going to enter a competition.
h. Paulo said that the exhibition had been fascinating.

B **Rewrite as reported speech.**

1. Paulo: I'm hungry. _____
2. Mum: I went to the cinema yesterday. _____

_____

3. The visitors: We enjoyed our visit to the museum. _____

_____

4. Emilia: The sculptures are amazing. _____
5. Oscar: I touched the dinosaurs. _____

C **Complete the speech bubble in each picture.** Use direct speech. Then rewrite the speech bubble in reported speech on the line below.

1.

Pablo said _____

_____

2.

_____

_____

Lesson 3 Reading

A **Skim the first paragraph of the text.** What does *MIM* mean? Then listen. 🎧 TR: 7.2

_____

MIM

About the Museum: In the centre of Brussels, in Belgium, there's a very beautiful building. It used to be a famous shop, called 'Old England', but now it's a famous museum, the *Musical Instruments Museum*, or *MIM* for short. It has a collection of thousands of different musical instruments from all over the world. You can see pianos, flutes, guitars, drums, bells, **electronic** instruments, mechanical instruments, even instruments made from bones! And of course, visitors have the chance to hear as well as see the instruments. There's also a fantastic library, a concert hall and a **workshop** where musical instruments are repaired.

MIM, Brussels, Belgium

Information for Visitors: On Tuesdays to Fridays, the museum opens at 9:30 a.m. and closes at 5:00 p.m. On Saturdays and Sundays, it opens half an hour later, at 10:00 a.m. The latest you can buy a ticket is 45 minutes before closing time. The museum is closed on Mondays. There's also a restaurant in the museum. It opens and closes at the same time as the museum.

It's easy to get to the museum by train because it's only 200 metres from Brussels Central Station. Cycling is also a great way to get there, and there's a place to leave your bike right next to the museum.

B **Read again.** Circle the correct answer.

1. MIM is _____ .

   a. a shop in Belgium   **b.** a museum in Belgium   **c.** a museum in England

2. You can _____ the musical instruments.

   a. play   **b.** buy   **c.** see and hear

3. If a musical instrument is broken, it might be taken to the _____ .

   a. concert hall   **b.** workshop   **c.** library

4. Opening time on Wednesdays is at _____ .

   a. 9:30 a.m.   **b.** 10:00 a.m.   **c.** 4:15 p.m.

5. The museum is closed on _____ .

   a. Saturdays   **b.** Sundays   **c.** Mondays

C **Choose three words from the box.** Write a sentence using each word.

| electronic   fossil   lucky   sculpture   sign language   workshop |

_____

_____

_____

A Match the direct speech (1–6) with the reported speech (a–f).

1. 'We're looking at fossils,' the teacher said to the students. _____

2. My friend said to me, 'I touched the sculpture.' _____

3. My friend said to me, 'I want to touch the sculpture.' _____

4. My friend said to her dad, 'I slept near a blue whale.' _____

5. My friend said to her dad, 'I'm going to sleep near a blue whale.' _____

6. I said to my dad, 'I had a great time.' _____

a. My friend told her dad that she was going to sleep near a blue whale.

b. My friend told me she wanted to touch the sculpture.

c. My friend told her dad she had slept near a blue whale.

d. I told my dad I had had a great time.

e. My friend told me she had touched the sculpture.

f. The teacher told the students they were going to look at fossils.

B Rewrite as reported speech using *told*.

1. 'It's cold outside,' our teacher said to me and my friends.

_____

2. 'I won't be home late,' said my dad.

_____

3. 'I'm playing football after school,' Carlos said to me.

_____

4. The teacher said to the class, 'You can watch a film.'

_____

5. 'We touched the dinosaur's teeth,' the children said to their parents.

_____

C Listen to the conversation. Then complete the sentences. Use reported speech. 🎧 TR: 7.3

1. Lina told her grandma she _____ exhibition.

2. Youssef told his grandma he _____ with his friend.

3. Amir told his grandma he and his friend Leo _____ at the sports centre.

4. Fatima told her grandma her teacher _____ in the world.

A **Complete the chart for a diary entry.** Use the information below.

lots of gold in lakes and caves   Visit to the Museum of Gold in Bogotá!

Seeing the exhibition 'Working with Metals' was so cool!

ancient Colombians used gold   met a museum guide and learnt about their job

Title? _____

Facts I learnt? _____

_____

Interesting event? _____

_____

My favourite part? _____

_____

_____

B **Use your chart from the Unit 7 Writing Lesson to help you write a diary entry.**

_____ to _____ in _____ . _____ told

me / us that _____ . I / We learnt about _____

_____ . _____ told me / us _____

_____ . It was really _____ . I / We _____

_____ and _____ . I was so _____!

My favourite part of _____ was _____ .

_____

_____

_____

_____

_____ .

VALUE

Be curious.

A **How curious are you?** Read the situations and choose the best answer for you (a, b or c). Then look at the information in the box below.

1. A new science museum has just opened in town. You _____
   a. go as soon as you can and spend a long time looking at the exhibitions.
   b. go and look at one or two things and then go home.
   c. go but spend all your time in the café.

2. You have the chance to go and dig for fossils. You _____
   a. dig for a while but give up when you don't find anything.
   b. stay at home. You're not interested in fossils.
   c. do some research about the fossils you might find so that you're well prepared.

3. Someone's going to show your class how to make chicken ramen. You _____
   a. join in. It's always interesting to find out how to make things.
   b. decide you don't want to join in. You would prefer to buy chicken ramen from a shop.
   c. stay at the back of the room. You'll watch, but you're not sure you want to make it yourself.

4. Your teacher told everyone they could go and touch the sculpture in the park. You _____
   a. go to the park and look at the sculpture.
   b. go and touch the sculpture. You'd like to know what it feels like.
   c. go to the park and stop at the café. It's too far to walk to the sculpture.

Give yourself points as follows:

Question 1 a: 2 points, b: 1 point, c: 0 points; **Question 2** a: 1 point, b: 0 points, c: 2 points; **Question 3** a: 2 points, b: 0 points, c: 1 point; **Question 4** a: 1 point, b: 2 points, c: 0 points

Add up your points. Then read the information below.

0–2 points: You're not very curious. You could try to learn more about new things – you might find them more interesting than you think.
3–5 points: Sometimes you're curious, but not always. Remember that things often become more interesting when we learn more about them.
6–8 points: You're very curious! You want to learn about everything, and that helps you enjoy life!

B **Tick three things you would like to learn more about.** Write about what you could do to learn more about the things you ticked.

☐ art ☐ computer science ☐ cooking ☐ creatures ☐ fossils
☐ history ☐ musical instruments ☐ space ☐ sports

8 Our Beautiful World

Lesson 1 Vocabulary

A Complete the clues with the new words in bold from Unit 8 of the Student's Book. Then complete the crossword.

1. A _____ place is very comfortable and often expensive.

2. If you have an _____ to do something, you have a chance to do it.

3. Something that's _____ isn't unusual.

4. When the sun comes up, it's called _____ .

5. Someone who's very good at something is _____ at it.

6. We can say '_____' when we're not sure about something.

7. When there aren't any clouds, the sky is _____ .

8. When you _____ , you enjoy yourself and don't do anything stressful.

9. When the sun goes down, it's called _____ .

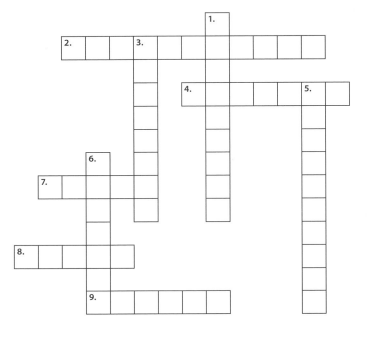

B Listen to the podcast. Write T (true) or F (false). Correct the false sentences. 🎧 TR: 8.1

1. It's 4,620 metres high. ___

2. Mount Sinabung is an ordinary mountain. ___

3. It's part of the Ring of Fire. ___

4. When the volcano erupts, it sometimes looks like sunrise. ___

5. The airports near Mount Sinabung stay open even when the air isn't clear. ___

6. If the air is clear, it's an opportunity to get a good view of the mountain. ___

Mount Sinabung seen from Surbakti Village, Karo, North Sumatra, Indonesia

A **Match the situations (1–6) with the wishes (a–f).** What does each person say?

1. Hans wants to take a photo of the volcano, but the air isn't clear enough. _____

2. Ellen needs to fly home, but the airport is closed. _____

3. Lisa would like to relax after school, but she has to study for an exam. _____

4. Jay can't play tennis, but he'd like to be able to. _____

5. Nadya and Katya haven't got a cat and would like to have one. _____

6. Ben is very thirsty. _____

a. 'I wish I could play tennis.'

b. 'I wish I had some water.'

c. 'I wish the air was clearer.'

d. 'I wish I could relax after school.'

e. 'We wish we had a cat.'

f. 'I wish the airport was open.'

B **Look at each picture.** Then write their wish in the speech bubble.

1.

3.

2.

4.

C **Complete the sentences with your own ideas.**

1. I wish I could _____ .

2. I wish I had _____ .

3. I wish I didn't have to _____ .

4. I wish my family _____ .

A **Scan the text.** Answer the questions. Then listen. 🎧 TR: 8.2

1. What's the Palacio de Sal? _____

2. What's it made of? _____

The Salar de Uyuni

The Salar de Uyuni stretches for over 4,000 kilometres across the southwest of Bolivia. It is 3,656 metres high, and it's one of the world's most extreme **natural** environments. Millions of years ago there were salt lakes here. After the lakes dried up, the salt was left behind and it formed a huge flat area – called salt flats. Sometimes, nearby lakes overflow and water runs over the salt flats. When the sun – or the moon – **shines** on the water, it **creates** an amazing light, which can be seen from outer space.

Salar de Uyuni, Bolivia

The Palacio de Sal is an unusual and luxurious hotel that's made of salt. The walls and the floors are made from salt bricks and there are even sculptures made of salt. The views from the hotel across the salt flats are extraordinary. It's a great place for photographers – and for people who want to explore the salt flats by bike or with an off-road **vehicle**.

The Salar de Uyuni is certainly a fascinating place – but it's not just a tourist destination. An important natural material called lithium is found there. Lithium is needed for batteries; for example, mobile phone batteries. So, you never know, maybe the lithium in the battery in your mobile phone came from Salar de Uyuni!

B **Read the text again.** Write T (true) or F (false). Correct the false sentences.

1. It's in Bolivia, in South America. _____

2. The Salar de Uyuni is 6,356 metres high. _____

3. It was created a long time ago, when old salt lakes dried up. _____

4. It's possible to see the Salar de Uyuni from space when light shines on water on the salt flats. _____

5. The Palacio de Sal is an uncomfortable place to stay. _____

6. The material lithium is needed for off-road vehicles. _____

C **Complete the sentences with the words from the box.** There are two words you don't need.

| attraction | creates | hang out | natural | resort | shines | vehicle |

1. You can't walk to the town from here. It's too far. You'll need a _____ .

2. A _____ is a place where people can go for holidays.

3. When something is _____ , it's not made by people.

4. A(n) _____ is something interesting to do or see.

5. The sun _____ during the day but not at night.

A Complete the sentences with the phrasal verbs.

> get away   get up   go back   hang out
>
> look forward to   look up   watch out   work out

1. Cara needs to _____ at seven o'clock to arrive at school on time.

2. I like to _____ from the city and relax in the countryside.

3. When you go to the Amazon Rainforest, you have to _____ for snakes.

4. If you _____ a lot, you'll get stronger.

5. I always _____ seeing my grandma. We always have a nice time together.

6. Can you _____ what the word *luxurious* means, please?

7. We _____ to the same place on holiday every year.

8. I don't want to play tennis this afternoon. I'd prefer to _____ on the beach.

B Complete the conversations with the phrasal verbs from Activity A. There are two phrasal verbs you don't need. Then listen and check your answers. TR: 8.3

Lucy: Hi, Alicia. Would you like to ¹· _____ tonight? Let's go to the cinema!

Alicia: Sorry, I can't. I have to ²· _____ early tomorrow for an exam.

Felix: I'm going to the sports centre to ³· _____. Do you want to come with me?

Mike: OK. I need to exercise more. I'll go and get my bag.

Daria: What are your plans for this summer, Marta? I'm going to the beach with my family. It'll be nice to ⁴· _____ from everything and just relax!

Marta: I'm going to Paris to visit my grandparents. I ⁵· _____ once a year, and I always ⁶· _____ seeing them.

C Complete the sentences with your own ideas.

1. I like to hang out _____.

2. I never get up _____.

3. I'm looking forward to _____.

4. I want to go back to _____.

5. I'd like to get away to _____.

A Complete the chart about a travel brochure. Use the information below.

trek in the jungle, spot pink dolphins   Amazon Rainforest in Brazil

stay in a hotel in Manaus, organise trips to the rainforest

see the Amazon River and amazing wildlife   low-water season (September–February)

fly to Rio de Janeiro, then take another flight to Manaus

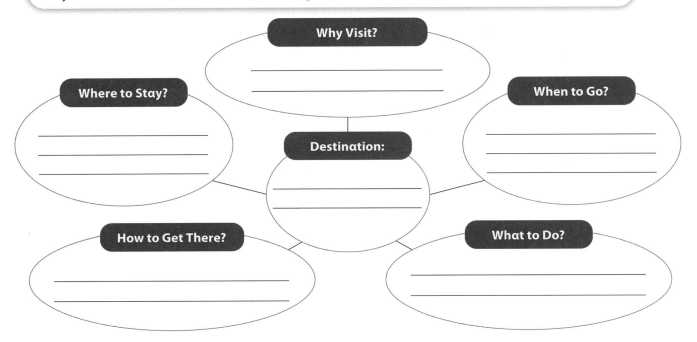

B Use your chart from the Unit 8 Writing Lesson to help you write a travel brochure.

_____ :
A _____ Place in
_____
Why Visit _____ ?
_____
is located _____ .
It's known for _____
_____ .

When to Go and What to Do?
_____
_____
The best time to _____
_____
is in _____
_____ .
That's also the best time to
_____ .
There are lots of fun activities
to do, like _____
_____
_____ .

**How to Get There and
Where to Stay?**
You need to _____
_____
_____ .

Some of the most popular
places in _____
are _____
_____ .

You can also stay _____
_____
_____ .

A **Read the list of activities.** Tick the five activities that help you enjoy the world the most.

- [ ] 1. Draw pictures of what you see around you.
- [ ] 2. Take photos of your country.
- [ ] 3. Learn more about plants and animals.
- [ ] 4. Watch videos about different countries.
- [ ] 5. Spend time listening to people talk about their experiences of the world.
- [ ] 6. Travel in your own country as well as in other countries.
- [ ] 7. Go on a long walk or bike ride.
- [ ] 8. Camp overnight somewhere and listen to the sounds around you.
- [ ] 9. Try food from different places.
- [ ] 10. Try new activities.

B **Choose your favourite activity from Activity A.** Write a sentence about why you think it is a good way to enjoy the world.

_____

_____

C **We often enjoy the world through our five senses.** Write sentences about what you see, touch, smell, hear or taste when you do the activity you wrote about in Activity B.

see	
touch	
smell	
hear	
taste	

A **Read the responses to invitations.** Write A (accepting), R (refusing) or MP (making plans).

1. I'm sorry, I can't. ___

2. Yes, I'd love to. ___

3. Where should we meet? ___

4. I'm sorry, I can't. I have to do my homework. ___

5. We could meet at the sports centre. ___

6. That sounds great. Thank you. ___

7. Thanks for asking, but I have to go home now. ___

8. Let's meet at six o'clock. ___

B **Read the conversation and circle the correct response (a, b or c).**

Tanya: Hi, Sasha! Would you like to go to the park after school?

Sasha: **a.** We could meet at the museum. **b.** I'm sorry, I can't. I've got football practice.
c. Yes, let's meet at five thirty.

Tanya: What about this weekend? Can you go then?

Sasha: **a.** That would be great. **b.** I'd love to, but I'm afraid I can't.
c. Yes, I can. When should we meet?

Tanya: Oh, good. Do you want to meet at nine thirty on Saturday?

Sasha: **a.** That sounds great. **b.** Thanks for asking, but I can't go on Saturday.
c. Saturday is perfect, but can we make it a bit later?

Tanya: No problem. Let's meet at eleven o'clock. Where should we meet?

Sasha: **a.** Let's meet at the café. **b.** I'm sorry, I can't. **c.** I'd love to.

Tanya: Great! We've got a plan. See you on Saturday.

C **Listen and circle the response you hear.** 🎧 TR: 8.4

1. **a.** I'd love to. Thanks. I'll meet you after school.
   b. I'd love to, but I'm going to Music Club after school.
   c. Sorry, I have to do my music practice after school.

2. **a.** That sounds great. Thanks for asking me.
   b. Thanks for asking, but I'm going to visit my cousins on Saturday.
   c. Thanks! Is it OK if I bring my cousins, too?

3. **a.** What time does the bus leave?
   b. We could meet on the bus.
   c. Let's meet at the café near the bus stop.

4. **a.** On Saturday afternoon in town.
   b. Let's go to the cinema on Saturday afternoon.
   c. At the cinema in town.

Cappadocia: Up in the Air

A **Listen to** *Cappadocia: Up in the Air.* **Circle the correct answers to complete the summary.** 🎧 TR: 8.5

Cappadocia is a popular place for tourists to visit in [1.] *North / Central* Turkey. You can see very old buildings inside [2.] *rocks / caves* in Göreme National Park. There are also more than [3.] *40 / 400* underground cities. You can see Cappadocia's rock formations from a [4.] *helicopter / hot air balloon*. To become a pilot you need to speak [5.] *one / two* foreign language(s) and know a lot about [6.] *science / history*.

B **Complete the sentences with the words from the box.**

> air   mushrooms   outdoor   protect   rock   thousands   tunnels

1. People have lived in Cappadocia for _____ of years.

2. Göreme National Park is like an _____ museum.

3. There are fascinating _____ formations in Paşabağ that look like _____ .

4. The underground cities in Cappadocia are connected by _____ .

5. Long ago, people went to live underground to _____ themselves from invaders.

6. From the _____ , the rocks in Cappadocia look even more amazing.

C **Read the sentences about Cappadocia.** Then circle the best definition (a or b) for the phrases in bold.

1. They have colourful paintings on the walls that look **just like they did** long ago.
   a. They haven't changed at all.   **b.** They have changed a lot.

2. In Cappadocia, **the real surprises** are below ground!
   a. The surprises are above and below ground.   **b.** There are no surprises above ground.

3. He says, 'Good communication skills **plus** a happy face is the most important thing.'
   a. You need good communication skills and also a happy face.
   b. Communication skills are more important than having a happy face.

D **Complete the sentences about the text.**

1. I was interested to learn that _____ .

2. I would like to find out _____ .

3. The thing I'd like to do in Cappadocia is _____ .

A **Match to form correct sentences.**

1. The visitors arrived at the science museum _____

2. They decided to _____

3. The museum guide asked them not to _____

4. They entered _____

5. They really enjoyed the film. They said it was _____

6. At closing time they went out _____

a. touch anything.

b. a drawing competition.

c. of the museum and admired the other buildings.

d. at opening time.

e. go to the art exhibition.

f. fascinating.

B **Circle the correct answer.**

1. We got up at 4 a.m. to see the beautiful *sunset / sunrise*.

2. You might see the northern lights if the sky is *clear / luxurious*.

3. It's wonderful to have the *opportunity / position* to relax.

4. If you become *ordinary / successful*, it usually means you have worked very hard.

5. I wish I'd booked a room in that *successful / luxurious* hotel. It looked amazing!

6. *Perhaps / Definitely* you should go to the art museum. You might like it.

C **Complete the sentences with these words.**

| enter | exhibition | go out | luxurious |
| perhaps | sunset | touch | unusual | visitors |

1. When you _____ of the building, you'll see the Photography Museum on the left.

2. Please don't _____ the statues or paintings.

3. _____ we should _____ the story competition. I think we could win.

4. The _____ about fast food was _____ but interesting too.

5. Most _____ at this _____ hotel love the food and the view.

6. I'd never seen a more beautiful _____ before. The colours in the sky were amazing!

D Rewrite the sentences as reported speech with *said* or *told*. Use the verbs in parentheses.

1. 'You can put your backpacks under the stairs,' the teacher said to the children.

   (told) _____

2. 'We've seen some unusual snakes,' said the explorers.

   (said) _____

3. 'I saw a fascinating exhibition at the museum,' Ali said to his friend.

   (told) _____

4. My mum said to me, 'You can sleep at the museum.'

   (told) _____

5. 'I'll meet you at the exhibition,' said my brother.

   (said) _____

E **Work in pairs.** Find and describe six differences between the two pictures. Say what the boy wishes he could do. Use the words in the box below and your own ideas.

climb	go	hear	learn	read	relax
ride	see	swim	take photos	walk	waterski

In Picture A, the boy wishes he could go to an island.

In Picture B, the boy wishes he could go to a treehouse resort.

Word List

Unit 1

breathe

competition

give up

great-grandmother

prize

race

rider

sign

stadium

take part

train

win

winner

Unit 2

biscuit

butter

delicious

flour

fork

honey

knife / knives

pepper

prepare

salt

spoon

sugar

yoghurt

Unit 3

acrobatics

act

audience

end

fairy tale

get married

king

life

lives

perform

queen

stage

theatre

traditional

trust

value

Unit 4

assembly line

burn

cardboard (box)

cool

denim

dye

dyed

fabric

glass (jar)

heat

look(s) like

metal (tin)

mix

pour

wooden (spoon)

yarn

Unit 5

artist

cheetah

creature

damage

disappear

environment

extinct

marine

protect

rattlesnake

scorpion

squirrel

Unit 6

gardener

lifeguard

marine biologist

mechanic

mountain guide

mural

painter

passionate

photojournalist

ranger

tennis coach

trail

wonder

Unit 7

admire

closing time

enter a competition

exhibition

fascinating

fossil

go out

lucky

opening time

sculpture

sign language

touch

unusual

visitor

Unit 8

attraction

clear

hang out

luxurious

natural

opportunity

ordinary

perhaps

relax

resort

successful

sunrise

sunset

CREDITS